Be HAPPY

Keys To Think Yourself HAPPY

K. LEE

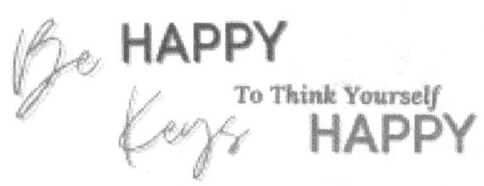

Published by Krystal Lee Enterprises (KLE Publishing)
Copyright © 2022 by K. Lee All rights reserved.
Please send comments and questions:
Krystal Lee Enterprises
services@KLEPub.com
sales@KLEPub.com

To Reach the Author:
Email: me@authorklee.com
Web: AuthorKLee.com Social Media: @AuthorKLee
770-240-0089 Ext. 1

Printed in the United States of America.
All rights reserved. No part of this book may be reproduced or transmitted in any form or by any means, electronic or mechanical, including photocopying, recording or any information storage and retrieval system without written permission of the publisher except for brief quotations used in reviews, written specifically for inclusion in a newspaper, blog, magazine, or academic paper.

ISBN: 978-1-945066-33-7

Dedication

First, I thank my Lord and Savior Yahshua the Christ for given me the insight and timing to complete this book. To my children thank you for your patience. To the reader, I wanted to write something that celebrates the happy go lucky people in the world. The people who always smile, laugh, try and help others lighten their load, and make the world a lighter place. Yes, happiness is a lot more than the state of being happy in a moment, in which I will explain in this book. May everyone be blessed by the reading or hearing of this text. Shalom.
K. Lee

Table of Contents

Introduction	7
Happiness Defined	13
Why Happy People	25
Ignorance Isn't Bliss	37
Guilt	47
Fear	55
Energy Vampire	63
You're not their God	69
Don't Judge Me	77
Don't Despair	85
You are a Vessel	93
Scripture that Will Encourage You	93
About the Author	106

Introduction

I wanted to dedicate this book to people who are serious about protecting their happiness. Yes, I am considered a very happy person, happy-go-lucky so to speak. If you speak with anyone who knows me even in the slightest way, they will confirm my personality to be as much. I was at one point known as the "Happy Coach" because I specialized in helping "happy people." I love being around people that have a happy character like mine. Two happy people tend to keep each other laughing and happy people keep the world happy, but what keeps happy people happy?

You know there is a lot of pressure on us to be the ones to carry the heavy loads for people around us. I know people don't always ask us, but happy people often can't help it. I know when I was growing into who I am today, I struggled with how to be myself when I see others—and the world for that matter hurting around me.

I went through a series of feelings, emotions, thoughts, and internal conversations that I think would benefit many of you. I am not an expert on happiness, but I am an experienced vet of happiness through some unprecedented circumstances. I will get into a few of those situations in this book. So, what is this book going to discuss in greater detail anyhow?

The first question I want to answer is why write a book on happy people? Aren't happy people already better off than everyone else? What I have found, is happy people are experts in disguising their true emotions. We tend to suppress the issues we may be facing so we can be strong for everyone else around us.

Although this quality at first sight seems admirable, it is truly damaging to the individual. You will find this person will someday explode and their actions are coming from a place of several years or decades of unresolved issues. So why happy people? Because happy people do have problems too!

We have heard that ignorance is bliss, but is that true? Happy people don't always find being ignorant of other people's plans for their bliss. Who wants to be a doormat or a constant catch-all for other people's problems—and do it with a smile on their face? How long before your happiness starts to whine down?

Guilt seems to be one of the number one nemesis of a happy person. Many people and life situations are quick to guilt trip you into believing you should be miserable because the circumstances around you are not happy. Although that may be true at times, there is a way to maintain your cool, better yet your happiness no matter your life circumstances. This not only is possible, but it should be your norm.

Fear is the kissing cousin to guilt. If someone

can't guilt trip someone into giving up their happiness, usually to control their decisions, fear is the next go-to. Fear is more than false evidence appearing real, it is an assault on your emotions. This sincere war against your equilibrium of peace is waged to have you make irrational decisions in split seconds.

A type of personality I had to learn to identify and I want to teach you as well to see is the energy vampire! These people right here constantly drag, tap, and suck the life right out of you. When they enter a space, it is like a cloud of darkness follows them. Whatever happy thoughts, unicorns, and hearts you were seeing, are chased away into the abyss.

Isn't it funny how everyone wants to be a judge, but no one wants to be judged? People are quick to throw out their two cents about you and everything around them, but are these same people open to your thoughts? How does this truth impact happy people? How can anyone be happy when they know the people around them don't value their opinion as much as their own?

I know with such hard realities around us, to know that our happiness is under attack by people we see and spirits we don't, how can we not fall into despair? Don't despair reminds happy people you are not here on earth to pick up the pieces for everyone else's life and neglect your own.

As happy people, we live our lives like coffee beans. We are not carrots! Don't be the carrot is a reminder that we are not to be shaped by our environments and life circumstances, but our surroundings are impacted by our essence.

Don't be a bully! People may ask how can a happy person be a bully. When we are surrounded by people who try to push us over, manipulate, and or control us, we feel the pressure to do something. Many happy people don't like feeling like sitting ducks waiting to be attacked in the silence of the night by a seen or unseen predator. Some of us are tempted to believe, that a way to protect our happiness is to get even or treat them how they treat us.

Another habit we tend to have is a savior complex. Happy people can take other people's happiness to the next level. Sometimes we want people happy more than they want to be happy. We try and meet every need and answer every problem, but we need to be reminded, "You are not their God!"

We are a vessel! You are a vessel. We carry things within us either positive or negative. Experiences, ideas, emotions, habits, etc. What are you carrying with you that could be blocking your keys to happiness?

If you carry hurts like everyone else, who can you run to in your time of need? Have you ever noticed how when you need help, many may not be aware or care? They say stuff like she will be alright, just give her/him an hour to cool off. These people don't know your loneliness. They don't understand your battle because your face wears a smile, your heart may be content, and the mind battles with the question, "Should you burden others with your simple problems?"

The question no one can ignore of course is what is happiness? Is it really just the state of being happy? Content with the things happening around you? Are you loving what is going on or lying to yourself saying all is well when it is not? Before we get into the juicy stuff, allow me to lay a foundation for genuine happiness. After all, that is what this whole book is about.

This book is inspired by a video series I created called "Keeping Happy People Happy" to watch it or learn more visit DrKrystalLee.com or connect with me on social media on any platform at: @authorklee (YouTube, FB, IG, Tiktok, TW, Clubhouse).

FB, TW, IG, TikTok,
Youtube:
@AuthorKLee
AuthorKLee.com
DrKrystalLee.com
Me@DrKrystalLee.com
Info@AuthorKLee.com

CONNECT ON SOCIAL MEDIA

Happiness Defined

Thanks for turning the page! Now let's dive deeper into the infamous question, "What is happiness?" You know the word we hear thrown around seemingly in every category of life. Many use happiness as a reason to fall out of unions, relationships, commitments, promises, and the like. I have a video series on being happy and I am now publishing a book on the very word, so there has to be a lot to be said on such a small 5-letter word.

Have you defined what happiness is or only defined what happiness means to you? Is happiness so subjective, relative to your life's circumstances that you can make good bad, and bad good? How many people really know what happiness is and can it be so easily defined? Happiness has a bad rap I feel because many people avoid life lessons, or just delay them under the guise of being happy. Happiness doesn't make you a runner it makes you alive and in the here and now!

Funny, because you and I know, some people say happiness or happy people don't live in reality. True happiness is something that dies off like our childlike imagination as we get older. When we start to realize that there aren't a lot of things about life, that's, well, happy it should fade. Problems are happening in our world true enough, natural disasters, issues in our families, even within ourselves. How can anyone be happy with the war raged on happiness?

It is a constant battle to understand and learn what true happiness is because we may believe we must settle for happiness being limited to being content with what is happening now. True happiness is so much bigger than a moment or moments of bliss. We all know a moment is gone from one moment to the next. Is happiness that flighty? How can anyone catch a butterfly that disappears in midair?

The plight for happiness is like searching for a unicorn in a pool. We are overwhelmed and overcome by the certain moving and shifting of the matters around us, plus we must remember to breathe to stay in the fight. Who then can search out a unicorn? Happiness? It seems like more pressing issues will fill in the time like water finds a home in every crack on a sinking ship.

But happiness is not as elusive as we may believe. Happiness is not avoiding reality or sticking your head in a fantasy that keeps you from dealing with life. It is a constant confidence that no matter the circumstances you will find a way to go through it! Although I may be afraid, I will not run away from my problems. I will not pretend my reality isn't real, but I will choose not to allow my current state of being to dedicate my joy!

Happiness and joy are not as easily interchangeable as one may think. Joy is a constant state of happiness and stability. Joy is not so quickly blown into the wind never to be seen again. You do not outgrow joy, because joy is something that is imputed on you from a place I pray many more people find. I would be misleading you if I could conclude that divine happiness as it was intended can be accomplished without JOY!

Joy can have you smile through your tests and even when someone talks sideways in front of you, with joy, you will laugh! Joy is a powerful undertone, not usually spoken of, but if joy is missing happiness is not genuine. Happiness is deeper than smiling all the time. Laughing more than you cry or even having an approachable mannerism. It is about the stuff within you that attracts those in a low state of mind to a higher one. It is JOY that makes you glow, live free, and truly be happy!

Yes, as many things are happening all around us, and most are out of our control. Feeling disconnected from power is more than possible when looking at the world from such a depressing vantage point. This point-of-view is beat into us from social media to the news. So how in the world, can you be happy when so many unhappy things are happening in the world? Well, I want to tell you the simple definition of happiness. Happiness is simply being happy and content in a timeframe that could be for a second, a moment, or a lifetime.

But how do you know that happiness is defined appropriately with its depth and then further know you've attained happiness for yourself? How can you do that? And then do you want to look like the happy people walking around smiling and laughing for no reason? A better question, if you don't do that are you happy?

Happiness is not just smiling, laughing, or looking happy, it is a deep-seated joy that is pumped through your conscious from a source greater than yourself. With that being said, how many of us are really not happy, right? I had to realize that all the times in my life I wasn't smiling, didn't mean I wasn't happy. Some of those times I was focused. I was hopeful or I was determined. At points in my life, I didn't laugh but I was happy, in that I had joy that never departed.

When I had solutions and was left praying for the next move, I still could find my joy and say I was happy in the depth of happiness. However, at the time, I was not very happy about the current circumstances. Yes, you can be happy and not be happy about the current circumstances. Many have heard the dialogue, "Hey beautiful, are you single?" She replies, "No, I'm married." His rebuttal if he is looking for trouble is, "But are you happily married?"

Women often think of what they are currently experiencing in their marriage to define all of their feelings. She thinks nothing of her wedding day at that moment, all the great things he does, but if she is currently happy in that moment with him. She then responds with her "yes" or "no." A wise wife knows, there are happy moments that include the sun and the shade. There is a happy marriage that each day isn't all sun sometimes it is rain, but how beautiful is the rain when the sun pops through the clouds!

Happiness is not so easily defined as a physical or emotional attribute but a state of being as we get older. We realize as we mature happiness is a deep-rooted understanding, a consciousness, that surpasses your current circumstances and draws you to a contended— stable point of view. Happiness is a decision. Happiness is not something someone can make you. It is somewhere you decide to be!

Because I laugh a lot and yes, I'm laughing right now as I write this book. Not because I am happy but because my JOY is feeding my happiness into overdrive. To think of what this book will do in your life, your family, the church, and the world, brings me incredible joy! It makes me happy to know that my current circumstance, time spent, is not frozen in time but living. My happiness is alive and well and will surpass my last breath. Can you imagine living each of your days with this vantage point?

Yeah, I may at first glance look like a person many would say is living in a fantasy because I am upbeat, smile a lot, be welcoming, and laugh a lot; but all of my life has not been happy. I have experiences and I am sure you do too, that would make a moon feel like a nightlamp amid a non-ending horror film. One that sees no daylight for the whole movie, and it is not till you reach the end—and you pray your character is alive, to feel the sun and hear the happy upbeat music welcoming a change of tide.

But a lot of happy people may not necessarily

look like me. Happy people are living in reality, and they realize their struggles, but the secret of your joy is your superpower! I know I live in that reality. My joy fuels my happiness to be constant no matter what life brings to me. I understand that problems are happening in the world. I also understand there are some that I can control. There are many more that I cannot, but what I've also had to come to grips with is there's something called a sphere of influence.

There is an area and a space in your life that yes, you do control. Your happiness is a choice, and I choose to be happy today, I choose this. And choosing to be happy isn't just a thought that comes into your mind, and you say it, and suddenly it's true. Choosing to be happy is a process. It's about what you're actually doing not simply saying. Happiness demands action.

I love it when people say, and I've heard this from Dr. Turner of KOGM, "You know, compassion with no actions, is not compassion at all." And I want to tell you, "Happiness, with no action, isn't happiness at all." You will never be happy if you are waiting for a person to make and keep you happy. To be happy, you must do the work and put in the time to make you happy.

Anything you start is a challenge in the beginning is it not? A new routine makes all of us sing the blues and "woe is me song." What happens after you keep working at something new after a week, a month, a year, 5 years, 10, or 20 years? You get better and that new thing is no longer new but second nature. You do what you have practiced for so long in your sleep and you can go on autopilot and end up right where you should be. Happiness is a decision you must be comfortable practicing to master, achieve, and thrive in.

It is an outlook, a way of life, and you make decisions (take action) to protect that happiness. With this understanding of happiness, it is not a toddler's version of happiness. Everything will go your way and you will never hear the word, "no." It is the opposite, you will hear no and maybe even often, but you allow the "no" to guide you to hope for an expected end. Imagine if you got everything you wanted to be so-called "happy"? How many of us would be lonely, depressed, heartbroken, unhealthy physically and emotionally, or beyond?

Who would admit, that our current state of being is because we got what we thought made us happy only to find it killed our JOY? We lost our power to fuel our happiness. We thought we were happy then to find out, we were not genuinely happy. We were only enjoying the moment. The time when we thought we got what we wanted. Don't allow happiness to be watered down to mean you get everything you want, but that you will get everything you need.

I love the promise I have, "No GOOD thing will I keep from you." Isn't it pure JOY to know that everything happening to you is a good thing for you to grow? Everything happening in your life will be used to take you from glory to glory, elevating you beyond your imagination. I can tell you I have surpassed my imagination for what I thought I would look like in 5 or 10 years. Surely what brought me past my thoughts, is greater, bigger, and more loving towards me than I am to myself!

My eternal happiness, fueled by joy is not autonomous phantom power, but it is my source and connection to a greater love. This source and LOVE itself, is going to make you proactive to want to change the lives of people around you; but you start with your own life. must find a way of getting peace in this world within you before you can share that happiness with others. You must be anchored in JOY to be able to fully embrace happiness and accept the challenges it helps you to overcome.

There will be challenges and moments in your life that can take your breath away. How do you find happiness, and joy, when your current view is a window showing you hail, rain, thunder, and lighting outside your window? How do you live through these moments or consider the thought of happiness in the time of grief, pain, loneliness, or disappointment? If everything in your life seems chaotic, uncontrollable, you are inconsolable, or know genuine happiness escapes you, consider implementing the tips at the end of each chapter.

I do know—some people say, "I don't have time to be happy," or "No one is really happy in life." I can tell you, "Yes, you can be happy. No, not everyone is in denial and living a miserable life." Do we all have challenges yes, but they don't have to make for an unhappy ending. If you spend your life chasing happiness, you won't find her. Happiness is not found it is created. You can make happiness right now, in this reality, and in this time and space. Happiness is something you build on a solid foundation.

What's your foundation? Your feelings? Other people's actions? What's happening in the world, on your job, with your children? Have you noticed something? Most people define happiness as things that are happening outside of them. Things that are not happening because of them necessarily, but to them. We cannot control how other people will treat us or what goes on in other people's hearts and minds, but we can work on how we receive or reject those actions. We can control what we give our time to and who we allow to suck up our space, energy, and happiness.

If you want to be happy, the first key is to learn happiness starts within you. Happiness is not about finding someone or something to give it to you. It is about learning what already is and having a strong foundation. To be honest, my foundation is rooted in scripture and Yah's (God's) presence. I have shalom (peace) and joy in life because I have confidence in God (Yah).

I don't worry myself about every little thing, who did me wrong, who will do me wrong, who's lying, or trying to get over on me. The schemes and plans of people in the world, governments, political offices, etc. I know and understand there is an equalizer, and He oversees everything hidden and public. I cannot control systems, but I can make and take actions that will move the system. I start with prayer for direction and stability in my execution of mindset, and then I put the plan into action.

Happiness is my decision, and my choice moves me to action. It doesn't move me to apathy, hopelessness, despair, powerlessness, or anything resembling defeat. It makes me triumphant in knowing the battle will be won because His promises are sure to me. His word will surpass my life and the ends of the earth! So, if He says He is going to do something I believe Him. Trusting God has erased my anxiety to control the world. I don't try to control people because I learned trust is more powerful than limited and finite control.

Keys to Happiness:
- Happiness starts within you.
- Find an inner stability that will sustain your JOY.
- Happiness doesn't happen to you it is created by you.
- Happiness has more depth than a temporary state of being, it's your constant confidence and state of mind.

Now use these keys and unlock new doors to happiness in your heart, mind, body, and soul!

Bye-bye for now.

Why Happy People

I used to think I was good because I could smile through anything. I could smile at a person I know hates me and it did not bother me. I was so above other people's thoughts about me, and my decision to smile, it over road any response I received in most cases. I thought because I could smile through anything I was in good—no great shape! I realized over time sweeping feelings and issues under the rug didn't make me brave or happy.

When I became a certified transformational coach, I often thought about my potential client. I asked myself, "Krystal, who is your targeted client? If you could select your clients, who would you say is your ideal client?" At first, I didn't know how to answer that question. Often when you start a new business you are happy to get any client, right? I quickly learned, that trying to target every group can make you miss your intended group. I wanted to be intentional in seeking out my clients. I also wanted to find clients that are looking for me.

So, my answer didn't come to me immediately but was discovered as I continued to live. I realized, in some areas of my life, I could benefit from a coach. I didn't picture my clients in my head or pinpoint what their desires might be. I started with wanting to help people stay motivated to start something new. I have always been a consultant, and accountability partner, but this was supposed to be something different. I thought I had to jump outside my wheelhouse to be effective. Little did I know, that my best clients were people like me.

My clients I decided are happy people. People who have problems, but they fight through the tears. They can find joy in pain. They can keep trusting God even when it looks like all is lost! I had to honestly ask myself, why do I need a coach? Or why would I need outside influence if I feel either completely myself or have a pretty good, happy attitude? I thought my attitude and demeanor meant I was good, but I was wrong.

Humanity was created by the Almighty Creator to interact with His Spirit of course but for each of us to connect. We were all created with community in mind. If I can only be happy because I am alone, isolated, or sheltered from the world, wouldn't my happiness be superficial? If our only sense of happiness steams from looking happy we miss the benefit of having others—even opposing forces in our lives. God, the Creator Himself, the great I AM, has fallen angels to contend with for our confidence.

Yah (God) doesn't allow all the wrong in the world to kill His plans for you and me. It is His will for us to have the fullness of Joy. For us to prosper and be in good health. For no good thing to be withheld from us—and yes that includes your happiness. Again, happiness is not about smiling and dancing about bad things happening. It is about trusting that even this will work for my good!

That ought to make you happy that you cannot lose in life even if you feel like you are. In the darkest of nights, the light shines the brightest. Your happiness can light up the darkness around you. Pushing the darkness further and further away from you. Happiness is yours, but you have to know that it belongs to you; and is yours for the taken.

So how do we strike that balance in life to keep our continence when so many things around us are intentional—or hell-bent on seeing us fail? The devil is hellbent on taking God's children captive. He wants to steal our joy, peace, happiness, dreams, and virtue—but don't give it up! There are things worth fighting for and your happiness under the right context is worth it.

The haters, accusers, naysayers, those that are envious, jealous, and the list can go on set against you are there to sharpen you. Friction can start a fire. Two forces going in opposing directions can work to make you stick your feet in the ground more or see the error in your ways. Iron sharpens Iron, so how can you grow unless there is opposition? Why would you change course unless the course you are on hurts more than the change?

It is human nature, or at least societal norm, to take the path of the least resistance. We know that the world is set against the things of God, we by nature cater to the 7 deadly sins than any pillars of virtue. For example, when someone wants to sell a new product to consumers, do they come together and put out a nice pamphlet explaining the benefits and cons of their product? Are commercials set on you appreciating differences between persons, social groups, and economic status to create a frenzy to encourage buying power?

Media uses sex to sell just about everything from books to food, movies, houses, drinks, events, candy, and the list can go on and on. Modern-day television is two clicks from soft porn and tv programming is closer to porn than television! However, what does this friction do? How do problems, situations, and life circumstances such as these make for a happier person?

Problems push us to define and redefine our happiness. This is not to make us unstable, flaky, or constantly quitting and restarting. The opposite is true, to make us elevate and grow to newer depths of happiness and joy. As we mature in our happiness we find, that anything can be thrown our way and we can still have a reason to smile.

I remember attending my niece's funeral. My niece was a gorgeous 16-year-old young lady who was always good at making you laugh. She had a contagious ability to make you empathize with her even if you knew she had some wrong pointed in her direction. She could pull you in and make you dislike or feel she had been wrong for a necessary correction. She was gifted and would have made a very convincing lawyer.

So my niece went into cardiac arrest twice due to complications with diabetes. She was in the hospital for a day before she was pronounced dead, but there was a fighter still within her. We were told she couldn't move, and that she had left her body, but I knew that I had come to see her for a reason. When I heard that she had been admitted, my sister was so strong, that I didn't realize—none of us did that she was heading to a place of eternal rest.

My sister told me to hold off on coming because we remained hopeful, she would stay with us, but the next day the opposite was true, and the doctors told us to prepare. I remember praying again and asking God, to give me the strength to come and to be there for my sister and my niece. I wasn't sure what was going to happen, but I believed all things were possible.

As I traveled to the airport, waiting in security, got on a plane, landed, fought to get my rental car, and drove to the hospital, I was happy. This was one of the hardest life situations I faced to date at that time, and I wasn't sure if I would be able to smile, laugh, or take my focus off of praying for life to come back to her body. When I pulled up to the hospital, I greeted the front desk still as myself. I am a chaplain, so I was able to come after hours to visit her, and I don't think they knew I was her aunt. The attendee at the front desk offered to give me a tour of her room and chatted with me the entire way.

I ended up saying a prayer for him and his family. He thanked me and asked as he was leaving, "How did you know the family" and I told him, "She is my niece." As I entered the room, I didn't burst into tears. My sister was fast asleep along with her fiancée Seth, a great man who loves her so much. I went to my niece's side and grabbed her hand. I prayed for her, but I put Yah's will above my desire. I know what would have made us happy, to see her walk, talk, and be Syeda!

But if God had a different plan, am I only focused on my version of happiness over what may make God happy and the world happy in the end? We were all connected, and the next 48 hours were a powerful time for everyone in and around that room. People came to see her every day, facetimed, and shared their love. We didn't realize it, but her parting brought us together and many happy moments took place.

My sister woke up after I was there praying for my niece and ironically anointing her with oil. I didn't realize at the time I was anointing her for burial, I thought it was for her healing. It was my pleasure to be used by God, and it made me happy to know I played a part in her transition from this earth to the heavens. My sister too gave herself to be used by Yahweh.

We have all heard that when people are in a comma, like my niece, they can still hear and perhaps see although they cannot speak or move. My prayer this entire time, before I left and while I was here, was "for my niece not to live an eternity separated from God. If she is meant to leave this earth, Father, let it be into your perfect arms that she finds eternal peace."

My sister joined me by her bedside. We talked about her being young, laughed about the silly things she did, and said, and surprisingly we didn't cry. My sister asked me, "Krystal do you believe she is still here?" I responded, "I do. I don't believe God put it on my heart to be here if it was too late for Him to do what He planned." We talked about salvation and if my niece Syeda was saved. She told me about how she was searching for God, and, ironically, this is how she found Him.

I told her, "We are saved by confessing Yashua is Lord over our lives in spirit and in truth. If by spirit we make our confession, her not being able to speak would not impede her ability to be saved now." My sister and I were holding my niece's hands, and my sister led my niece to Christ as she lay lifeless to the naked eye, but something happened in that room.

I had anointed my niece's feet with oil and she did not move. Nikki, doctors, and others touched Syeda and she did not move. However, as Nikki prayed with my niece, she moved her entire shoulder off the bed! She moved her feet several times to her touch. She even moved her head during the prayer. Before this prayer and after, she did not move anymore.

Joy, to know, the happiness I felt, cannot be described. Yes, my tears still came, my heart still ached when the plug was pulled the following day, and even though I did not like the circumstance, I was happy. I was happy to be there for my sister, see my sister walk her daughter through the salvation prayer, and then see my niece move her last movements. I saw her the first day she was born, and I saw her the last day she was on earth.

Her life and death challenged me and redefined happiness for me—elevating me to a place I didn't know existed in God, Yah. It is the standard for the young to bury the old, but another thing for the young to bury the younger. My heart grew that day. I cared more about people who intentionally choose to skip their medicine because of other life situations encouraging them to subconsciously lean towards suicide.

Happiness wasn't only found in the smiles she gave, and the laughs she created, but I am sure it was also in the peace she felt when she left. She hated diabetes and none of us could understand the depths of her hate until we realized she didn't want to return. It is still a process to accept Syeda's and God's wishes. He has a way of making everything work to His glory, life, and death to finish a perfect work in each of us.

Yes, happy people have trying circumstances that can rip our hearts out, and change the tune of our song, but there is JOY that comes in the morning. Sometimes joy doesn't tarry, it comes now! Joy is not only what comes through for us, but angels, people, friends, and family help us make it through tough times. Community is necessary to experience true happiness.

Christ is our biggest confidence in that the Word was made flesh, so our words take on life! When the accuser comes and tells lies when people say this or that is not possible when we are presented with a problem, whose words do you believe? Some would not pray for their children at that moment because they believed the person was dead already.

But we know, that when Yashua went into the room of a girl who was dead, who He said is not dead but only sleeps, He called her name and she got up! If she got up, she heard Him. If we are His children, called by His name, then when we speak, we tap into His Spirit. It was by spirit we spoke to Syeda in that hospital room and that is required to be saved. It is not about the words we say but in spirit and truth that we must believe to be saved! How amazing that even the mute can seek repentance and salvation, and find it! I was happy!

The haters in our lives, no matter their shape or form, push us to focus more on defining our happiness. It makes us see the depths of being happy. It is not limited to a state of happiness, or liking what's happening, but a layered understanding. When people don't like you, don't let that break up your happiness. Don't allow people who can't stand your joy to make you feel self-conscious about being happy. Don't hide your joy, or believe you hide your joy because you withhold a smile. You can be happy and not smile.

Happiness is a state of mind, a determined decision made with true intentions not to give up. A key to happiness is knowing that your existence impacts the people around you. You are not in the world isolated to your island. You are a living breathing vessel that can change the atmosphere around you! You can make what was intended to be unhappy, joyful, laugh, smile, and lift other people's spirits with your conscious decision.

Before my niece was unplugged, the Father had me pray and the prayer was a reminder to us all to love each other. To stay connected not because death has come, but because love should have never left. We are happiest most when we feel valuable, useful, and helpful. How can we be these things if we isolate ourselves from our families, friends, co-workers, and the world? We must live in community and start our happiness within, then shine it outwards.

In that room, we all cried yes, but we laughed, smiled, gave apologies, admitted faults, and took the time to clear the air about matters including and excluding Syeda. That moment was a joyful time, and one I will never forget. The feeling I felt, sharpened my joy, my happiness. No happy moment can replace the extreme emotions I felt in those moments of my life. Her funeral is a hard second, but I know the goodness of Yah even more now than ever before.

I am grateful for this period in my life, although I wouldn't ask for it, nor wish it on anyone. This is living, to know that someday there will be an end. So live and learn to be happy, and content, in all circumstances. I didn't think it, but we need to be sharpened so that we can cut pain off others. If we are dull, we cannot cut anything but only hack, saw, and pray to tear something free. We do know that this process will not be done with precision or a clean break.

I want to encourage you to think about the most intimate times that have shaped your life. They can be moments where you liked what was happening or you hated them. These experiences shape our lives, but they don't have to keep you from being happy! Life, rains on the just and the unjust. Weather changes from day to day, but your state of mind can be fixed on seeking joy.

Make that decision today, to eat the meat and spit out the bones. You don't need the bones and don't accept trashy words, dead things with no purpose said to you or about you. If there is some truth to something someone says, put it into perspective. Don't let it tear you down but build you up. Yes, my niece may have been dead in the body, but her spirit was alive! She was only sleeping. Yes, some things in your life may be dead, but in the spirit, they are alive! Speak to those things and watch the Word live through you!

Keys to Happiness:
- Your existence impacts the people around you.
- Learn to eat the meat and spit out the bones.
- Address difficult moments in your life and decide to be happy.
- You don't have to like the circumstance, to see the value in a struggle. Some of our biggest chances to be happy stemmed from a moment of deep pain.

Now use these keys and unlock new doors to happiness in your heart, mind, body, and soul!

Bye-bye for now.

Ignorance Isn't Bliss

I commend everyone who has lived through a hard test and didn't tuck their hand in the sand! You know, the people who refuse to live in reality. Happy people can live and do live on earth. We are not unicorns, but we are people with struggles similar to you. The biggest difference between a happy person and others is our decision to be happy. We have to work towards happiness. Happiness doesn't just manifest, it is created.

Are you creating happiness in your heart, mind, body, and soul? Are you creating happiness in your home, at your job, or your church? Are you a beacon of love, joy, laughter, smiles, and kind words? Or are you a resounding gong singing the words of what someone used to be, should have been, could have been? Are you the dark shadow that everyone tends to avoid unless they have an ear for gossip?

Have you noticed how much ignorance has really hurt you over the years and did not create bliss? How many decisions can you think of in this split moment that would lead you to say ignorance is more like hell than bliss? Or to say, "If I would have known back then, what I know now, I would have done 'x, y, z'."

The Word says, "My people perish from a lack of wisdom (knowledge)." People are dying because they do not know how to maintain a constant, stable sense of being during the storm. When the storm was raging around about Jesus (Yeshua) on the boat out at sea. The disciples saw Him sleeping and I paraphrase to say, "He doesn't care if we live or die. How can He be sleeping when the storm is raging like it is?"

I am sure they wanted to wake Him up and behoove Him to deal with the storm more aggressively out of their own fear. Only they didn't know what He could do to the storm. They didn't know he would say, "Peace be still," and the raging storm would cease altogether. For all they knew, he would secure the boat, bark orders, panic like them, or say a prayer before they all perished.

After Yeshua spoke to the winds, the waters, the boat, everything went calm. He said, "Ye of such little faith." Why do we have to see everything stop in front of us to believe that everything, yes, even the chaos is under His control? If He looks like He sleeps, don't think it means He can't hear, see, or is absent-minded about what is happening on Earth. Nothing comes to God the Father as a shock.

Yeshua says I can only do what my Father tells me, so if God the Father is leading Yeshua, the Word, what are we to fear? He tells us to fear not. To keep our shalom, peace, joy, happiness. Our confidence should be in Him not in our abilities. Some argue, that if you believe in God for real, meaning practice what you preach, you are not in reality.

It is amazing how if you are not carnal, you are outside of this reality. You live in a fantasy world, one with flying fish and swimming unicorns. The spirit realm is free and things that may take time to manifest in the natural can be materialized in moments. What you say in spirit can bring things from heaven to earth. We can bind and lose things with our words.

There is a power stronger than any unicorn we tap into when we are not ignorant of the power locked into our words. What can you accomplish when you make your hands and feet utensils under the power of Yeshua? Who is under the authority of God the Father, Yahowah (Yahweh)? Being ignorant of the enemies' devices is not bliss but bondage. How can anyone find happiness in bondage? This is not forced bondage but willful submission.

Sometimes our happiness alludes to us because we don't know it belongs to us! Many of us have dealt with great suffering and pain. We associate good things being followed by a slew of bad things. We see great things happening and that makes us fearful instead of joyful. It is like being happy sends a signal for the minions of destruction to come and take it away.

A key to being happy is to not be afraid to be happy. I know there is an unspoken word, a code, that men are not supposed to smile. Smiling in some cultures is a form of weakness. How stifling is that? Can you imagine taking wedding photos and in every picture, the man looks miserable because he must look strong, Gansta, unbreakable in the photo? When you don't smile, you can look morbid, blank-faced. Does that make you feel love, appreciation, and harmony?

A smile gives off a vibe, and some people are ignorant of how body cues impact the soul. When you feel the love written on someone's face, it can bring immense happiness. You can reflect on that moment when a person asks you "Are you happily married." Even on your worst day, you can honestly say, "Yes, I am happy. We are not perfect, but we are perfect for each other."

There is power in being happy. You can impact the world around you because of your presence. You can change a tide and quiet a storm with your words. You are better than a unicorn, you are real, walking, talking, and using your power for good. You are emulating the happiness the world wants to see. Many won't ask you how you do it, they instead become your hater or spectator. They wait for you to fail at something so they can laugh at you.

Ignorance truly is not bliss, because when these same people, go through what you did and respond very differently, they will then revisit their judgments of you. It is at that time they want to know how you stay happy. What made you smile when all they could do was cry? What pulled you out, when they wanted to crawl up and die? How can you take a licking and keep on ticking with joy in your heart? They think it is magic, but no it is work.

Happiness is a working relationship between joy, love, and peace. We know that joy comes from the

Lord and that God is love. We know that Jesus (Yeshua) is the Prince of Peace, so your happiness is locked into God the Father, the Word, and His Spirit intermingling with you. It is in our weakness He is made strong. When we try to fight with our strength we tire out and pray for Him to intercede.

As we mature, we realize, the more I try to save my life, I lose it. Yet, if I were to lose my life, in that I make Yah the governing power over my life, I am saved. This ignorance of not knowing that true power isn't in trying to control everyone and everything, but realizing even if I did control many things I cannot maintain it always is a hard truth.

We can have someone's heart today, but that doesn't necessarily keep them from what they may decide to do tomorrow. We must choose each day to love, be happy, and keep the peace. Not everyone will feel that way of course. On the flip side, can there be bliss if you avoid experiences intended for you to grow as you journey through life?

God is king in setting rules on how to do this or that. Many hate rules because they are uncertain about how rules protect you. Many instead of being content with being protected want to know from what. Then they want to know how that works, then why, but to what end? The more questions we ask, the more power we will desire to make our own decisions. When we make our decisions, we take into account the knowledge we have and then believe we are more intelligent than God to make the call.

When God told Adam and Eve not to eat from the Tree of Knowledge of Good and Evil. Eve wanted to know why not. Then she wanted to know what were the pros and cons. Then she decided it would be better to eat the fruit than to follow God's command. She didn't stop there because she reached out to Adam to have him join her. They both decided to defy Yah and do what they felt was best.

How often do we allow our sense of happiness to defy God's command? Then after they made this terrible decision, were the two of them happy? When they were eating the fruit, getting the knowledge, did it please them? How long did that last before they realized they were hoodwinked? They lost it all because they were tricked and seduced into disobeying Yah. Now, all of humanity must deal with this dilemma and battle to obey God or rely on our knowledge to lead and guide us.

It's not about not knowing, sometimes we know but we are ignorant about knowing. We are not all clueless about the things that happen to us especially when they are right in front of our eyes. Sometimes it hurts too bad, or we are lazy and may be afraid to say something. To say something would point to our reaction, response, and if there is not one. What does that say about us? So, for many of us sadly, pretending we don't see it is a workable solution until we must address it.

The sad part, so much about life can pass before then. Matters can wax worse and problems that could have been small issues become colossal. Don't tuck your head in the sand and expect things to go away on their own. Ignorance—even pretend ignorance is not bliss. It could cost you much hurt and pain. It is better to deal with the harsh realities and determine how to maintain your happiness.

Again, happiness is not about enjoying the moment or being happy in the current state of things. Trust God and believe that at the next step and the one after that, He will lead you to where you ultimately want to go. When we look at the world with a renewed perspective, we can appreciate our life circumstances. Why wait until you are out of the storm to realize the storm took you in the right direction?

We must learn to be content in all situations and that comes through trusting that "this too shall pass". Everything is wrong, and the right things may still change. Change doesn't have to be the enemy, it can be seen as part of your growth! Growth may not feel good but where it leads is up to you. People perish from a lack of wisdom, other translations knowledge. The knowledge of good and evil is something men still find difficult to judge.

Knowing our limitations as humans, with fragmented experiences, with both painful and beautiful histories, does shape our reality. Thank God He is bigger than all our problems, situations, and experiences, there is nothing under the sun He has never seen, heard, or experienced! He knows us in more intimate ways so we can trust that all things work to our GOOD for those called according to His purpose who love Him. Our happiness—joy is our strength.

You can make it through any test and keep your shalom—peace because you know, this situation will work for you no matter how it may look and feel right now. Wise up to the enemies' plans, and come to the understanding that life is filled with rain on the just and the unjust. Storms come and go, and problems or tests are sent to test your faith, trust, and understanding.

The Bible tells us, that God would not have us ignorant of the enemies' devices. If being ignorant was bliss, why would He want to show us our real state of being when living in a false sense of consciousness about ourselves and the world around us could be sufficient? Ignorance can cost you everything and keep you oppressed even when no one is holding the chain or has locked the door. The doors are open to happiness, but you sit in a cell moping about what was, not seeing what could be. If this is you, update your perspective and change your trajectory!

If there are things in your heart, mind, body, soul, on the job, in your business, or inside your relationships that need to be addressed. Don't put it off anymore, but explore solutions, options, and support to bring you through a trying time. People were made for community. Community with each other but most importantly with God (Yah). He can change any direction, calm any storm, and make a way out of no way. Trust Him…

Keys to Happiness:
- Nothing lasts forever, the good, bad, and challenging. Things pass away—change. You steer the direction.
- What is your point of view? Being fearful about the test, or seeing beyond it?
- All things work together for your good, for those who love God and are called according to His purpose.
- Knowledge and wisdom, gives you power. Trusting God maintains your happiness.
- Running away or pretending does not make problems resolve. Choices and actions do over time.
- Avoiding matters will not guarantee you happiness, they only prevent you from acting. At times, the longer you wait the more you push away your happiness.

Now use these keys and unlock new doors to happiness in your heart, mind, body, and soul!

Bye-bye for now.

Guilt

A true nemesis closely followed to your happiness is trying to make others as happy as you. Most of us when we are trying to learn and maneuver this beautiful circus, filled with color, the unthinkable, unplannable events that happen in life. We have learned to smile or laugh to help lighten the pressure we feel when a dark cloud comes over us to rain.

We don't look at the clouds and pout—usually, we laugh and start dancing in the rain! Others look at us and wonder I am sure, "Why is he /she so free? Why are they dancing in the rain? They could get sick, catch a cold, mess up their hair." The list could go on and on for why a person shouldn't dance in the rain or find joy amid their pain.

The joy, you have on the inside of you, tends to bubble over, doesn't it? I remember I was in Vegas when I was 18 years old for a production convention. I loved the time in the city. I ate good food, went mountain climbing with my classmates, and went to a few networking mixers with my class. I even walked through a few casinos and saw the desperation on people's faces to win back their rent and watched others happily playing slots without a care in the world.

I was already happy and bubbly, so the scene didn't shift me to want to play. Even now when I come to Vegas, I don't gamble because it doesn't spin me in either direction. I am neutral. At one of the mixers I attended, I was having a great conversation with a production director from Virginia. He was pleasant and jovial. We talked for a while and he was impressed by my smile. He kept saying how it never seemed to fade when moving equipment, helping out, or speaking to others.

When I tell people I am all smiles practically all the time, they doubt it. If I tell them, I love to laugh, they think I laugh to please or stroke their ego, but really—come closer, I just love to laugh. We talked and laughed as a group and he told me, "Krystal, if you can bottle up your energy and sell it you would be a billionaire."

"I said really, you think so?"
He said, "Yeah. I wish I had some."
Then I asked him, "What do you think we should call it?" We pondered for a minute and I said, "Bubbles!"

We both started up laughing again and continued our conversation on production, cameras, equipment, content creation, and all that jazz. I guess I am still a nerd at heart.

I was thinking then and still do to this day, how I could pour my energy, spirit, laughter, joy, and lightheartedness on others. At 18 I felt that way, and when

I was younger, I had an overwhelming desire to help save the world and bring joy! I wanted people to be happy. As an adult now in my 30s, I still tell people this and I mean it. I have found, however, that not everyone is as genuine about seeing others happy or appreciating my desire to see them happy.

Some people see the heart we have and they desire to exploit us. This exploitation can be intentional or not, but the impact and the way it tries to tear us down are the same. Guilt. Have you ever been around someone who could ask you questions that feel like they are prying into your heart and soul? They don't go to these questions to get solutions, but to stir up your emotions. To bring that heavy cloud they may feel upon you—not to share the load so that a solution can be reached—but really because misery loves company.

These people will attempt to guilt trip you into sitting in misery to give them company and then complain about ya'll's condition then work towards no solution! It is one thing to have problems and share them so that you can get the help you need, but to wallow in your pain and bring others down—then hold them there is cruel. Happy people by nature are people pleasers. We go the extra mile to prove or show our love and we don't mind doing it.

We tend to be the ones in relationships that do the most. We come up with ideas to celebrate our commitments. We write letters, send videos, encourage you to laugh, and make light of life's complications. Some people see this gift and guard it because they cherish it. Then others see it as a form of weakness. They try to pressure you into decisions by using their misery as a weapon.

They want you to exchange some of your joy for their misery but disguise it as you not being empathetic enough. They say things like "if you really care you would" do this or that. It doesn't have to be a marriage or relationship. Guilt can be used as a weapon on jobs, in comedy skits, and at the grocery store. Have you seen the people that will cut the line and of all the people, they pick to cut in front of you? They see you smiling and looking happy, so they think, because you are happy you won't mind them jumping ahead.

Maybe on your job, people assume you are free or don't mind spending time covering their shifts because "you are so great with the customers." I remember being a server back in the day and I seemed to get the craziest work schedules and my managers would tell me, "We know you are a team player, and we can put you anywhere." I had 8 tables before and all kinds of stuff, because they felt I could just "handle it." Yet, I am human like everyone else! I used to think to myself.

I would feel guilty about leaving on time at work because this person was running late. Honestly, I had to get to a point where enough was enough! Yes, I have a happy agreeable demeanor as I am sure you do too. I would love to help people and as my mom would say give the shirt off my back to help someone else. Then I had to realize, what makes their life so much more important than what I want to do with mine?

Why are the things they had to do, more important than the things I want and plan to do—no matter what it is? Too often people want to know why you say "no" to them. Not so they can understand and get to know you, but so they can judge if your no is acceptable. I had to realize, that if I said "no" to a request, I didn't have to have an answer as to why.

Sometimes, we should lean on our mother's old saying, "Because I said so." We don't have to explain ourselves to everyone all the time why we decide to make a decision. We have one God to be accounted to and other people are optional. When I realized I could be happy and say "no," I started putting more boundaries on my time with people.

I realized I had to start guarding my happiness like I expected others to. No, I didn't and still don't want to let people down, but I also know, I cannot be the only reason a person stands. They must use their own power, strength, and desire to stand. Another hard lesson, I can't be a lifetime crutch or doormat for anyone, and you shouldn't either. Many people will walk all over people they feel are resilient. What I find funny, those same people will cuddle a person they think is fragile.

Not sure if the approaches are from fear of causing untreatable harm, having regrets, or just not wanting to be bothered with a meltdown? Happy people go through rough patches all the same and guilt is like a dagger dug into anyone's heart that stands in the way of it. How do we dodge it? Fight it? Overcome it?

Think with clarity and be slow to move. Too often we are Mister and Miss Fix It. We want to come in and turn a rainy day into a sunny day in people's hearts. We want to impact relationships, change the mood, and make people laugh, but there is a time for everything under the sun. A time to laugh, cry, morn, etc. We have to respect people's emotions even if they are not what we choose for them. We need to be careful not to force our joy on others, but let it shine.

When we move quickly to save, we can find ourselves in unfamiliar territory. We can think our attitude, positive outlook, or approach to life can pull people out of a rut. We even believe we can take people out of depression. Make them see what we see about them and in them. The truth is no one can make another person do anything they don't choose to do and participate in.

Sometimes people do need to be alone, and sometimes they need more than our love. Allow people time and grace, and don't feel discouraged or think you have lost a battle because someone didn't respond the way you had hoped. Don't allow not only people to guilt you, but the devil either. The devil is the worst accuser. You know the thoughts that come into your head that tell you things you should feel, think, or do that are contrary to what you know is right?

Our enemy is just not guilt itself, but it is those using guilt to manipulate our emotions to get us to make bad and impulsive decisions. Guilt had some of us buy cars, co-sign for stuff, go places, do things, and the list can go on and on for other people. Then when we feel the brunt of those decisions, here come little nymphs in our ears whispering how we deserve to be here because we tried too hard. Or that the world will never appreciate us or what we bring, so stop trying.

What I love about God is He can drastically change your life from moment to moment and day to day. You can make a dumb decision now and do better in an hour. Surely falling angels hate that you can change your mind. Don't let the enemy, a bad relationship, manager, or anything else make you feel compelled to make habitually bad decisions.

Some of us picked wrong. Wrong car, wrong house, wrong state, wrong college, wrong spouse, wrong god, but that doesn't mean keep going in the wrong direction because guilt is ushering the way. Fight the urge to bend to guilt and coercion disguised as giving up. You deserve better.

Keys to Happiness:
- Guilt is manipulation used by people, spirits, etc to usher bad decisions.
- Feeling guilty can be the reason you don't say "no" when you should. So you can't say "yes" when you want.
- Your happiness is something you must guard. No one should make you feel guilty about that.
- Having a heart to please others shouldn't make you a doormat but a servant leader.
- Servant leaders lead by example. The advice you give, you should also be quick to take, and to help others you must help yourself.

Now use these keys and unlock new doors to happiness in your heart, mind, body, and soul!

Bye-bye for now.

Fear

If guilt had a loud and obnoxious relative, Fear would be it. Fear is something that gives you the stanky eye, and talks loud without saying much. Intimidates without a second thought and pushes many to make absolutely horrid decisions. Yes, fear is that deep weight that falls in your stomach and makes you lose your appetite. If you can't see straight, think straight, worry—fear creeps in.

Many know fear, also known as false evidence appearing real to many of us, encourages us to think and worry about things that may never happen. It is the what-ifs that we play out in our sinister imagination that leads us to this despair. This weighted room with a ball and chain that imprisons us to walk around lost, confused, broken, and a slave to the loudest voice calling our name.

Fear creeps into our mind when we are weak and can overtake us making us think irrationally and programs us to do irrational things. These irrational split decisions are made of course at the drop of a dime. You know that fear flight syndrome that we all go through in our psychological processing? Should I go, or should I stay, what will happen if I leave? I don't know, so I stay.

How many people stayed on jobs that they outgrew years back only to dangle long enough to be fired and replaced without a second care? People who knew they picked the wrong spouse, but out of fear, they thought they couldn't do better and settled. Those who won't let people go that they know are out of their league, because they don't want to feel the rejection. To know the reality, that they are the one who is truly blessed not the person they berate and put down daily. This is not just for women, I have seen and heard many cases where men are the ones being abused, put down, and disrespected, but no woman would encourage another woman to endure the same actions.

Fear of being judged because they may be clergy, pastoring a church so they live with Jezebel because to admit the fault may cost them everything. Their perfect bubble will explode, and then implode, what would they be without the fantasy life they created? How many men I know don't have the guts to fight for their true happiness but will settle to listen to a nagging woman—not even a wife instead of finding a Proverbs 31 woman?

They are afraid to be alone. Women are not the only ones with internal clocks pushing us to make unsettling choices about our future. Men are making those hard choices too and not everyone's choice is for the best. Just look at the relationships, jobs, colleges, careers, and plans you have made out of fear. How is that turning out for you? The answer should prove why fear needs to be dropkicked out of your life!

I remember when I was 18 years old. I was working for a media company, a TV channel in Orlando Florida. I was so blessed then as I am now and landed a 4-year degree position by happenstance. I was grateful and I enjoyed the ride while it lasted. I remember talking to a pastor whom I respected tones, Billy Crone. I was watching so many of his series at that time and I was getting scared about my future.

Have you ever read things in the Bible and it didn't make you want to go outside and live, but stuck your head in a book, locked the doors, stayed home, and prayed everyone out there gets well? He was doing a study on Revelation, and I was overwhelmed. I used to want to be married, have children, and live the white picket fence dream. However, the more I lived, and studied, I felt my desire for family dwindling. I no longer could picture a wedding. I saw hell and the gates of heaven. I wanted to be sure I went and encouraged others. I wanted no one to be left behind.

At the time I was dating, and I had an idea he would propose, but I had no idea what to say. I loved him, and under different circumstances, I would without hesitation say "yes" if he asked me to marry him, but I was scared to live. Pastor Billy told me, he said, "Krystal, what were the people doing in the days of Noah?" "I said they were living life." He said, "They were eating, laughing, getting married, having children, and everything you said you wanted. Don't stop living life because no man knows the hour of Jesus' return. So, if you want to get married, get married. You want children, have them."

I never forgot that conversation and after that day, my fear subsided. I could see myself getting married again and I was excited. I realized I could share all my ideas with my husband and children. This love I had I could share and not let fear make me bottle it up and through it in the basement. Are there things in your life that fear has made you bottle up and cast aside?

I saw that day how fear was handed its walking papers. That loud voice that shouted political fallout, racism, marginalization, failure, social class, economic status, and credit score, was completely silenced. Nothing stood in the way of what I intended to accomplish. I knew then, everything I needed to win, I had. To beat fear, you must believe in something that calls your name louder. You must focus on a bigger agenda that is real to you. Caution is warranted, but what we fear most are things that won't actually happen. Some of the most fearful thoughts are spiders crawling all over your body. Feeling the breath of a dragon on your neck or standing in front of God—if you did that in the flesh you would die because He is so holy. After death is an entirely different matter.

Again, none of these things will likely happen and that's why I say, you got to learn how to manage fear and park it in its place. Happiness and joy lean on trust, faith, and confidence to ward off fear. Perfect love casts out fear. Love something, someone. I loved the guy whom I was afraid to marry. We got married and had a beautiful baby girl. I don't regret it, but I would have regretted not doing it because I was afraid. Kayda is my oldest child, and she has done wonders to make me a better woman, mom, friend, and all-around person. What if I missed out on loving someone who would show me so much in return?

That love cast out the fear of the unknown for how I would provide, take care of her, and know when she was hungry, sick, or tired. As a new mom, I was winging it and love was my anchor. I had family, friends, and of course God, but I was in that room with her every day and loved it! Love made me overcome my fear of failing, messing up, and missing the mark. Love doesn't care about your age, race, or where you are going, and it doesn't care about where you've been.

The Bible tells us God is LOVE. When we love others, we are demonstrating God's character on earth! Fear is no match for God, for Love. Fear has one objective, to crush you, to destroy you to curve your sound decisions, and to make you irrational. Nothing good is going to come from fear, because fear is a means of control. Fear wants to control and dominate how you think, feel, reason, and live. Fear wants to be the god of your life.

Fear again is no match, but many are worshiping a heartless beast that will run their entire life into the ground. Bondage is all you will be entitled to if you let fear run wild in your life. God gives us freedom, liberty, and peace of mind. Fear cannot thrive in peace but in chaos. Learning to settle your mind, worries, and anxiety, is key to beating fear. Getting alone where you can think, relax, and reflect on good things, is key to trusting the process.

When you become fearful of taking that leap for a new job, you have to remember how you were kept in your current and older jobs. When you worry about how you are going to make it forward, consider how you made it this far. When the Hebrews were leaving Egypt and long after the occasion, the Bible references the acts of God for His people. He reminds them continually of His goodness towards them. He instructs us to take communion to remember His Son's sacrifice and what He gave for us on Calvary. Why?

The reason is, there is power in trust, confidence, and faith in God. Faith can move mountains. Faith grows not in fear and doubt, but in faith, trust, love, and peace. This is not a fake peace, but one you can feel, see, taste, and touch. Yah's presence can wrap around us making us feel a heightened sense of peace that we don't want to come down to base reality. We fight to stay in this state because we feel powerful and fearless there. It is like listening to battle music, that gives you the energy to keep your momentum.

Don't let fear win this fight for your soul, which is your power, will, and emotions. Take back your happiness, maintain your joy, kick fear in the butt, and let peace, trust, and love reign.

Keys to Happiness:
- God is Love and Love casts out fear.
- Fear comes to bring you into bondage. It wants to be your god. People who use fear are only workers of that spirit.
- Find peace by thinking about things that are good and lovely.
- Don't spend your time fearing the unknown, the unlikely, and what you cannot change. Pray about everything.
- Those who put their TRUST in God will not be put to shame. So, trust in Yah and try a new job, make a life change, and don't allow fear to hold you in places or positions you were never intended to visit.

Now use these keys and unlock new doors to happiness in your heart, mind, body, and soul!

Bye-bye for now.

Energy Vampire

Have you noticed how your energy, smile, and presence can impact a room? People like being around you even if they won't tell you because you bring life to what may have been a dead space. You bring fun, energy, hope, love, laughter and joy. Who wouldn't want to be around you, right? But some people have a different approach to life, the Energy Vampires.

These are the people who have nothing positive to say. When they see you, they complain about your happy aura and say I wish you didn't smile so much! These people know how to suck joy out of a room. Their power is not in making people better but in putting their thumbs on people's necks to elevate their own self-worth. They get a kick out of stirring discord and making people second-guess themselves and their actions.

Do you know about these people? They are everywhere but you can control how much of your time they consume and how you deal with them. These people are looking for easy prey. They don't want to be exposed so they work best in small circles sowing discord with the claim of honesty. What we all know, these people don't give criticism to be helpful and not everything they say is accurate.

These people feed on negative energy and a slight gap for a new idea to be planted, they go for the juggler. There needs to be an atmosphere to be caught by an energy vampire. What is that atmosphere? What makes you vulnerable to their plans and tactics? What makes you a perfect prey for a person dying or dead inside?

As of late, they try to make vampires look sexy even when they are washed out, malnourished, and the like. Who would have thought that would ever be sexy or attractive? Times have changed have they not? In this time and age, the gossiper has fans, a show, and an audience. Seems like society loves to suck the privacy out of people's lives and make fun of people's suffering. Energy vampires seek to prey on a host that breeds strong emotions within them.

They are attracted to the ones that have great promise and making progress. The people are one of many from their neighborhood, but they are the only ones to make it out! You would think people would put them on their shoulders and celebrate what is possible. Instead, they only see their shortcomings in their accomplishments. Instead of taking the balloons and floating them everywhere, they pop them to watch a person shoot in all kinds of directions. They expect you to fall back to the ground, back to earth, down to where they feel they are.

How do you dodge such intentions? How can you protect your happiness, joy, peace of mind, love, and kindness from people who see your presence as a threat? You learn to ignore the screams and whispers. You learn to eat the meat from a complaint or compliment and spit out the bones. You learn that people-pleasing is not on the menu.

You will not give your happiness, joy, and life's work to someone that will discard your carcass as trash after they have sucked the life out of you. You sacrificing your happiness did not bring them anywhere closer to their dreams. Their dreams are dead and have been dead for a long time. They need regeneration and that is bigger than you—much bigger! Breathe easy, not everyone will appreciate your accomplishments, happy countenance, and substance you bring to your life and those around you.

Keep radiating and watch them squirm watching you excel, going from glory to glory, and good to great! When you continue to be you, you are shaping the world around you to give the same energy you bring. You reap what you sow. What goes around comes around. As long as you are being you, you will get the opportunity to stay in that flow. When the energy vampires see your aura, they notice how starkly different your outlook is from theirs. What should happen, they should desire to know how you do it. Unfortunately, that is not the response with this breed.

They see you as a threat to their willful basting in discontent. The way you lose the battle is to change your mindset, lose focus, and allow doubt to kick in. These people will say stuff like, "You may be happy today, but let's see if you are happy tomorrow." We all know the secret though; it rains on the just and the unjust. We all have trouble, but how you make it through is the difference. When trouble comes, how can you sing in the rain and dance? You must believe that where you are going and headed is greater than where you come from. Even greater than where you are right now.

      This hope in an unforeseen but very real future gives you the energy not to quit. This energy is intimidating, it is unstoppable. Death cannot even stop its progress. It is a living, breathing, constantly adapting force. The energy that the falling slaves put into the earth for freedom, we are benefitting from right now. The same passion that the '70s, 60's, '50s, and '40s willed into being could not be stopped! But how it appears, what we believe about our progress, and whether we embrace it is another matter.

      Energy vampires cannot kill those whose light shines too bright like the radiating sun bursting star. They can blow the dust off empty and dead spaces. Bring new life, paint, and color, to what was once a grey, morbid, and dilapidated building. Some people can live and thrive in darkness, hiding in the shadows, the cold drafty places. Others, want the sun beaming on their face. To feel the light and airy movement of the breeze. Chase butterflies and even hug trees. Not in the literal sense but in chasing the peaceful and calming energy that comes from rest and confidence.

      Don't let the bloodthirsty vampires disgruntled with their progress or your presence leech off your happiness. Energy vampires will attempt to use guilt to make you feel bad about moving forward in life. They will use your emotions, struggles, challenges, or your imperfections to function as a counterweight to your progress. Don't let them bring your dreams down to Shaol. Faith and love overcome a multitude of sins. It can erase the pain and give you beauty for ashes. What was once dead, can be born again—live again.

Vampires don't know that it is your efforts that will someday pull them out of the slumps they are in when they change their approach to life. The same people talking about you today will be the people who celebrate you when you are gone. Why is that? Because pure happiness, joy, faith, and love is a force that even a vampire has to turn their head to acknowledge. Have you noticed in the films they try to block the sun, but the sun comes, and pushes out all darkness then there is no place to hide?

They may want to hide in your happiness, but they shouldn't be able to stay if they are a mole to your operation. Their black energy should not take root to block out the sun shining bright in your life. Create new spheres of influence and don't be afraid to create something new! Not everything old has inherited value. Some things are just long overdue for an overhaul.

Keys to Happiness:
- Don't expect the people who grew up with you to celebrate you but be okay if they do.
- Moving forward and having trials and failures is normal, but you need to be okay with staying focused through the process.
- Your future and where you are headed is more important than where you have been and where you are.
- Don't let the crabs in the barrel moonlighting as an energy vampire bring you, your happiness, joy, or dreams down to Shaol (stop your dreams).
- Everyone is not rooting for the person at the top, some want to pop your balloon to watch you flail all over the place. Know your true friends and watch the company you keep.
- Not everything old has inherited value. Some things are just long overdue for an overhaul.

Now use these keys and unlock new doors to happiness in your heart, mind, body, and soul!

Bye-bye for now.

You're not their God

Contrary to popular opinion, you are not responsible for another person's happiness. It is not your job to make the world happy, but it is your job to be true to yourself and protect your sphere of influence. To make it happen, it is best to link with like-minded individuals to ensure the space you create is happy. Happiness is a mindset, a way of life, and a presence you emit from the inside out.

If a person is not happy within themselves, they will never appreciate the happiness, joy, or God they see within you. They will only try to find the fault in you because they are aware of the faults within themselves. As a believer, I know that the spirit of Yah (God) lives within me and many are attracted to me because of Him. His character is LOVE and it is warm, comforting, and changes everything. Some see that on you, in you, and they want that for themselves.

They think that hanging out with you, talking to you, watching your videos, and buying your books it will miraculously jump on them too! These are tools to help people discover a balance in their lives that only works with their keys. Your key to happiness is not necessarily my key to happiness, but you seeing what my keys have opened for me will encourage you to explore your keys. Can you relate? Have you seen people you have admired so much that you wanted to be just like them? Only you couldn't, right?

You still had to be you and they were still who they were. Admiration is admirable, but wanting to put pressure on someone else to live your life and bring you happiness is too much to ask for wouldn't you agree? People in relationships, on jobs, in ministry, parents with children, or children with their parents, siblings, the rich to the poor and the poor to the rich, hear me. "You are not their God." We are not called to be a personal god to someone who loves something about you. We were never as people meant to fill the place of the Almighty God.

We were created for His reasons, to bring joy, love, and community to the world He placed us in to dominate. We were never intended to dominate each other, but to live in community with one another and God at the head. It is a struggle for man to understand and appreciate such a concept. We don't need someone to lord over us, we need to work with each other, equally sharing and appreciating each other's gifts. In this atmosphere, happiness can thrive!

When we realize our shortcomings of being God, we can move and point to the real power. We can show others the way is through Him and without Him there is no love. We can be shiny examples of His goodness, but the form of godliness we possess has a source of power. I had to learn a very hard lesson about what it means not to be God to the people around me.

I used to have a mindset to save, give, share—perhaps overshare to help people make it through tough times. I used to think through the challenge and work through several possible answers for them to choose. I soon realized they didn't want an answer or solution, they wanted someone to step in and take over and do the work that needed to be done. Many will see your energy and assume you have enough to carry out their life's work as well.

The real question is, "Does anyone have that kind of energy?" Can one person's faith save an entire nation if those same people intend to do nothing to bring it about? I struggled to understand why people I loved couldn't or wouldn't do the things I did to get similar results. I had to realize that my walk wasn't theirs. I had to be okay with them working through their success and failures. The toughest life lesson I have not yet learned is to watch my children repeat life's process.

We can work hard to prepare people to make the right decisions, but we cannot make anyone do something they don't want to. Neither should you allow someone to make you do something or become something you were never intended to become. It is a hard life living up to your potential. Can you imagine taking ownership of so many lives? We must move and allow people to make choices that can lead them to different paths in the same direction.

Some may arrive in 1 year, 3 years, 5, or 20 years. Does it matter, if they all made it? It may matter in time, but to know that in the end I win, does help me to deal with the life happenstances I see and live through myself. Be mindful of the difference between being helpful, a temporary crutch, and when you are the mule doing all the work as they shout orders from the sideline.

You are not a workhorse sent to earth to fulfill someone else's life quest. You were born for a purpose and time such as this! Chase the things you are born to do, and the relationships will build as you journey. People will come in and leave out. We must keep our hands open to receive and give like a live and active body of water. Water nourishes everything from man, beast, the skies, and to the earth. Let us learn from water to flow trusting the current God sets as a course for our life and travel the depths we were meant to go.

When people see you constantly moving, it is tempting for them to want to ride your current. If you allow them to, they forsake their own growth pattern. In addition, if you are not careful, you can lose your own purpose trying to give someone else direction. Be nice, and be happy, but don't allow others to make you their God. At first, it is flattering, even enjoyable for someone to call you and want your input. Then it transitions to demanding your time and energy. That then becomes a weight tied about your neck, feet, and hands. You cannot take a vacation without them calling and likely they were the reason for the vacation.

I see countless relationships of parent to child or vice versa where this tug of war of how the parenting relationship has to change when God steps in. Some are not ready to give the greatest influence on their life to God, and others enjoy their parents saving them at every turn. They may say they don't, but their actions prove otherwise. Sometimes you need to let them learn to pray for themselves. You must decrease so that God can increase in their lives.

Sometimes bills should go unpaid, and stuff gets turned off so that healthy spending habits can take form. Not every low place is meant for their destruction. Often, it is for their elevation. Be patient with them and yourself as this trying transition takes place. Taking that pressure off yourself allows you to be way more helpful and I dare say happy!

I remember when both my younger siblings needed help financially. It was to be expected, of course, they were young, new adults and trying to acquire things in life. I was happy to help when I got the first request. It made me feel good to think I was taking care of my siblings and stepping in, in their time of need. Then I started to notice a pattern.

When things flew off the rails in their lives, I would get a call. When their phone was about to be turned off, they were about to get evicted, their car repossessed, and the like my phone would ring. Funny, when I would call to give them advice on budgeting and how to do things, those conversations didn't seem to take the same presidents in their lives. My help didn't appear to be helping but holding them in a buying cycle that clearly didn't work.

They didn't see how their choices were impacting their life and didn't work because I was the backup. It was when I stepped back and started letting the phones get shut off. Saw people lose their cars, apartments, and have to switch jobs that I learned something. Saving people doesn't look the same way. Sometimes saving someone is allowing them the room to learn. I am not saying that we may not all need help from time to time because we do, but we must strike a balance to be effective.

Overly involved parents can be the biggest stumbling block to their children growing to be interdependent adults. Yes, they should be okay with asking for help, but not expecting people to do it for them. I have to be careful that I don't as we say "baby" my children because I handicap them more than I function as a help. Letting people learn to think through their problems and find solutions they want to try is critical to taking possession of our lives.

When we own our direction, we can appreciate the journey, especially when we win! We all love being winners, right? The truth is we all failed more times than we care to mention. Allowing others to win means giving them room to fail so that they too can learn what they need—in the way they need to for growth.

Keys to Happiness:
- Don't feel obligated to save everyone from everything.
- Learn your limitations so that you can appreciate other people's growth patterns.
- Your way isn't the only way they will survive.
- After you have done your job, allow life and God to take over.
- The best-learned lessons are personal.
  We can work hard to prepare people to make the right decisions, but we cannot make anyone do something they don't want to. Neither should you allow someone to make you do something or become something you were never intended to become.

Now use these keys and unlock new doors to happiness in your heart, mind, body, and soul!

Bye-bye for now.

Don't Judge Me

Boy, if I had some money for every saying I have heard, and I am sure you too, about being a judge, we would be rich. Everyone is a critic nowadays are they not? We have parents judging their children, and children judging their parents. Total strangers are looking at people and determining life spouses, assessing singing abilities, and determining stars from regular people. In all fairness, are any of us truly so gifted to be a judge of another?

When I think of a judge, it is supposed to be a person who is wise, balanced, and fair. With our life circumstances, can we be fair? Can we departmentalize our experiences from our jobs, feelings, or emotions? Often, we say people can sing because they give us goosebumps. Is that talent or an ability for someone to tap into your emotions?

Surely those with a 6th sense would say a spiritual component exists in our world. This element makes us feel and see things others do not. This realm for believers is more of the natural order than life itself. With a society full of judges, why do people take such offense at others judging people's actions in the respect of understanding what they like or dislike about someone?

I understand if you do not want to be judged, in the respect that another person has a say over your life. However, how can we argue that a person should not judge our behavior to determine how they want to interact with us? Is it not natural and spiritual to guard the things you value? You wouldn't leave diamonds on a shelf with the window open, blinds open, and your front door unlocked. You would hide them in places to protect them. You would watch out for suspicious behavior, and you would be prepared to defend something more valuable like a life of your own.

So, with such sacrifice, how could judgment not play a factor? We say things like "good judgment" and the word in this context can be overly simplified to mean choice. We should use good judgment when making decisions. This means we should weigh the details and assess the situation. When you hear, "I am a good judge of character." What does that mean to you?

I surmise you think, "I can watch, observe, and determine good or bad habits." I then know based on patterns I see, what conclusions I can presume true. Based on previous experience, and things you have heard, or read, we make decisions on how we will deal with someone. How close we will allow them to be and determine if we should be cautious around them. Judgment isn't the gavel slapping down and sentencing someone to a fate of imprisonment or freedom. Instead, it is about watching the behaviors of others and deciphering what spirit or spirits they bring.

It is over time you make decisions unless you feel like an expert in predicting the ending of a relationship before it even begins. If you have dated a person with a personality or characteristics you don't like, most feel if they see it again, they will recognize it and avoid it at all costs. Meaning, terminating relationships that remind them of a past they don't care to repeat. It could also mean, that someone may have characteristics, or traits, that are immature for what another is looking for in a spouse at that time.

Judgment is the ability to observe and reason, then make a decision based on your reasoning. Judgment is not a big scary wolf unless you do not like the outcome of how people treat you when they judge. Yes, some people do not judge fairly. In that, some people will not like or love you for matters beyond your control. That is an honest bone to want to pick with anyone. Then again, would you want to argue with a person to accept you, if you could spend more of your time with those that do?

Some would argue, segregation is more comforting for some than integration. They wanted equality they said, but they didn't want the discomfort of being rejected by those who thought them inferior. Having a unified cause can make people learn to put aside trivial matters to focus on the big picture. Martin Luther King was about the rights of blacks and minorities, yes, but he was moving to be about the rights of the poor including all persons within the category. I believe as a society we are going to shift more in that direction especially if you are a believer in Christ. Spirit and our affiliation with the Father should and does matter more than race and bloodline. Christ said to Himself, "Who is my brother or sister except those that do the work of my Father."

People love to say nobody can judge me but God. When I hear it, it makes me think of the scripture, "Those that don't believe are condemned already (John 3:18)." God has judged the world before it began and condemned sin, then nailed sin to the cross for those that would choose salvation. Judgment can be harsh because the repercussions can be so strong.

People ought to assess serious matters like having children with someone, getting married, starting a job, business, etc. with great care to judge accurately. These decisions are not trivial short-term results but often can shape the trajectory of your life. When people say "Don't judge me," or "Who are you to judge me," I say "You are right. I am not judging you; I am only deciding for me."

You can make choices for yourself and not put unnecessary pressure on someone else. Sometimes the true reason for why you won't decide in someone's favor may be the very thing they need to know, hear, and understand. Don't let people "boo" you out of making the best decisions for your happiness. Some people are simply not ready for you when they meet you. So, give them room to grow up to your level but don't stop moving. God is the only One that can redeem time and when someone gets desperate enough, they will try anything. Shame that God wasn't the first option, but it can be like that at times, right?

Another point I have noticed about those who say don't judge me or you judge too harshly, they already know what you are about to say. Likely, that person has already done the work for you in judging themselves. Many of them know something is wrong with them they just hope, pray, or think you should be with them anyway. The reasonable ones want you to be there for them through their transition. However, I would say that the ones who love you would respect you for doing what is best for you staying or leaving.

I know for pastors, hearing don't judge me comes from a place of hurt, shame, or resistance. People don't want anyone to judge them but God, so they don't have to see the downtrodden looks on people's faces as they walk through the doors. Then when they sit, the snickering that happens in front, beside, and behind them. I tell you, the person you want to judge you is God, but allow Him to use people He loves to correct you. Sound judgment is good for you. A just judge who holds the gavel can rule in the right favor for what that person needs. Not everyone needs to be released and not everyone needs jail or prison time.

As pastors, we are not to judge a person's condition to condemn them but to point out their errors to free them. Too often the heart of the church is misunderstood. We are to expose sin, call sin what it is, and point people to a better way through Christ. When King David had to choose who should judge his actions by counting how many Hebrews were in his kingdom, he said he wanted God to judge him because He was just. He went on to say that man can be cruel, and his enemies would pursue him until nothing was left.

When your parents judge you, sometimes it is not the punishment but the judgment in their tone. It is not what a person is saying but how they say it that makes your skin crawl. We all know we at times in our life fall short of the mark. What we all need is an open mind to grow. The judgmental tone is not what we need, but we can all use an understanding and open mind to point out the truth. Truth sets us free and can accomplish way more with light than the dark feeling that comes from unloving judgment.

Sound judgement sets us free but condescending and judgmental attitudes oppress more than they help. The key to judging is to select the right Judge who is fair and just, and then trust the process. God doesn't make mistakes, and he can use any vessel to accomplish His great work in your life. If you feel the spirit of offense coming up within you, or in someone else, breathe. Judgment is a part of life and decision-making. Just know, that to the degree to which you judge others, you too will be judged. How you treat people does matter and how they treat you all the same.

Don't be afraid to call a spade a spade, and to make good sound decisions.

Keys to Happiness:
- Judgment is a part of life.
- Be fair and a good judge because the same degree to which you judge others will judge you.
- Judging others is a byproduct of you making decisions.
- Don't be afraid to call a spade a spade.
- Many times, when people say don't judge me, they have already judged themselves. They know what you are saying and understand why you are saying it. It is your choice if you will stick around for their growth or grant them space. No wrong or right answer except what is best for you.

Now use these keys and unlock new doors to happiness in your heart, mind, body, and soul!

Bye-bye for now.

Don't Despair

It can be very discouraging to put your all out there and get nothing in return, can't it? Have you ever put your very best effort out there and it seemed like those who benefitted could have cared less? You know when you spend all day in the kitchen, cooking for two days for Thanksgiving or the like? You took the time to invite everyone to show up, but many did not come. Others come and wave a few times, grab a plate, cover it with foil, and then make a quick exit.

Did you wonder if your efforts were really appreciated or if you were just free takeout? It makes you feel like "Why do I waste my time doing anything for someone else?" Especially, if they do not care. I am sure you have also thought about how you could have done many things for yourself instead of others.

For those who are dating, I cannot tell you how many men are discouraged by the many relationships they start and end for a similar reason. I don't believe many are against treating the woman they invited out on a date. However, what many do dread is being used. When someone uses you for a free meal when the woman knows, not even the man's best foot forward would change their mind for that woman to want them, they feel used.

Feeling used can make you have a sour impression on dating or looking for the spouse you know deep inside you desire. This desire is overshadowed more and more by the fear of being used. Soon, you don't have the same heart as you look for someone special as you did before. Instead of you having a happy attitude towards your dating experience, you are mad about the money you spend. The time you appear to be wasting, and you are bitter, or discontent with the experience because you are lacking.

If you spend your money, time, energy, and effort, but you don't get what you seek it can be at the least frustrating. The truth many seek a companion because loneliness is very real. You date to find a companion, someone who can be in the moment with you. They move in the direction you are going, and together you can accomplish more than you do on your own.

How upset would you be if you are pouring out to not be alone, but all you seem to find, attract, or date are women that want to suck the essence from you, and your loneliness remains. The point for which you sought the women still draws a void, but now you are also depleting your resources for no apparent reason. I feel for men who know they are being used and therefore reluctant to date.

Likewise, women who are out looking for Mr. Right can be easily jaded with a few common problems. Dating in this day and time many find it challenging to find a man willing to meet their expectations.

Sure, people are wanting a unicorn, but most have rather simple desires. For the man to be self-sufficient, can commit when the time is right, be a man of integrity, and have a belief structure they follow is a simple standard.

If you were to ask many women today, they would say men have too many options, so they are in no hurry to commit even if they found Mrs. Right. Knowing that there is a slew of women to replace you at whim may make you feel a lot of pressure to adjust your expectations or face loneliness. Both are looking to fill their void, and they are both going through the struggle.

Loneliness hasn't reached its peak until you are in the room with others and darkness, emptiness and lack still looms. Don't despair when your efforts may look as if they fall on dead or bleeding hearts. I know the journey may be long and trying, but there is hope at the end of the tunnel. I remember one time on a job I worked, a co-worker struggled to feel appreciated by me.

At this time, I was a server, so as customary in this industry, you wait tables, and you make your money by the tips you collect. At the end of the night, you are expected to tip out the people who have helped you throughout the night like the bartender, busboy/busgirl, and food runner. Their tip-out, the money you pay them, is determined by you typically although amounts may be set as to what is expected.

She expected to make a set rate per person that

night, but I had a slow night, and I ran my own food; but the truth on that shift I did not have it. I gave her the tip based on what I made. Ironically our first names are the same, at the time we both had 2 children, but she had a set of boys, and I had a set of girls. Our children were even the same age at the time.

I went to give her the tip-out I had for her, and she refused it. She said she didn't want it and she should stop being so nice. To be fair, she was more than a food runner. She was a mover in the restaurant, and we all loved her for it. I didn't give her, her tip because I thought her work was shabby. I felt so bad after and even was a bit shocked because her response wasn't her normal character.

She was vocal about her tip-out and complaining about how people don't pay people what they are worth. It hurt my feelings because I believe in integrity, being honest, and appreciating everyone. This same person I have tipped out more than the requirement when I did well in previous weeks. So, it was trying to hear her say some things when I knew I had been good to her.

I tried to talk to her about it, but she was not trying to hear me. She was short, curt, and wouldn't let me get a word in. I felt despair because my integrity was poorly represented to me. What I decided to do, to make the situation better, was to pray. God said to invite Him into all of our problems. Sure, I thought this problem was small, but the impact was huge. During the ordeal, I could feel fear mounting up in my stomach. I could feel the cold loneliness of being isolated from being accepted and included.

     After praying, I was committed to continuing to operate with integrity. I didn't try and overcompensate but allowed my prayer to work on her and me. I didn't give her what she thought she deserved at all costs to make artificial peace that night. I was true to myself, and I could appreciate her feelings about the situation, she was true to her position.

     It was about a week later from that ordeal and I made great money that day and weekend. I gave her a tip-out as I did usually, based on what I made. She came to me, and she thanked me for giving her extra because she said, "I didn't have to do it." I responded and told her, "I will always give you what you are worth based on what I have." She thanked me for being the same and explained to me she had a lot going on last week. I figured she did because she was different than her normal self. Even happy people can have issues that take our minds and attitudes in different places.

     I let her know, "We all have things we are going through. I really do appreciate you. So, thank you." I didn't think she was my villain because she was doing what she felt best. We were not communicating then so we couldn't resolve it, but in a week we got it. When I thought to despair, I was rest assured, that two happy people may not always appear to appreciate each other. Two single people may get together and not communicate and they both live unfulfilled.

     Don't despair if a problem strikes in your life they are bound to happen. The key is to not let that problem make you change your integrity, core values, and attitude to do the right thing. Instead, let despair lend itself to making you understanding and willing to communicate so that the picture you do see is clear.

Keys to Happiness:
- We may not always feel appreciated or understood but don't despair.
- When you feel alone, lonely, or feel fear kicking in, don't let it influence you changing your core values, integrity, and attitude.
- Two happy people can make each other respond out of character when other outside factors play a role, and practice understanding.
- God wants to be part of the solution no matter how big or small you think the problem is, God cares.
- What may have been a broken relationship a week prior, can be restored when we continue to maintain our integrity. Understanding and compassion will weigh out in the end.

Now use these keys and unlock new doors to happiness in your heart, mind, body, and soul!

Bye-bye for now.

You are a Vessel

We are vessels that carry many things. We carry our experiences, hopes, and dreams. Prayerfully we are holding these items in our hearts and minds, and expressing them in our actions. We also carry a smile, personality, character, mood, and vibe that typically attracts or deflects what we are looking for.

It is an important key to happiness to watch what you carry in your vessel. What you think will become what you believe and shape how you live your life. If you continue to utilize the unpleasant experiences, you have had to pull you into a dark space, your results will be watermarked with a dark trace. If you can pull from your life and allow that to work as a tool to propel you forward, you are thinking about things that are good and lovely, that yield even better fruit.

We must remember where we come from so we can better appreciate where we are. While we are reflecting on our journey, it is not a moment to revert to what we came from, but to get more motivated to press towards our high calling. As we live and press forward, we will find many nuggets that give us the ability to live life and ideally find happiness along the way.

We are to keep our minds set on good things because those things help us to stay focused on what made us start or continue our journey. Other things we can carry in our vessel that are in fact counter-productive are guilt, ignorance, fear, bad company, regret, shame, and biased judgment. A sure sign to kill your chance at being happy is to keep things in your vessel that do not create the soil to bring forth desired fruit.

If you want to be happy, find joy, and keep a steady attitude that has learned to be content in all circumstances, you have to rid yourself of these enemies. You have to remind yourself of the choice you must make to be happy. This conscious decision means you operate like a coffee bean and not a sweet potato or carrot. Both are hard structures in their natural states. But if you put them in water, the weight of challenges and trials of life causes the water to boil, and they will become mush under the pressure. The sweet potato and carrot are no longer strong, but soft, and have been shaped by their environment.

The coffee bean on the other hand has shaped its water to give more energy and life. The coffee gave more and still maintained its integrity, or state of being. When the cares of this life are thrown at our minds, other people's opinions, etc, we must flavor the water. We have to understand, it is not all about what is being said or done, but what we choose to do about it. When we find out we are being used, abused, ignored, tolerated, hated, or dismissed, how do we choose to respond?

No one can do to you what you do not allow. At some point in this relationship or engagement, you have to agree to the terms set before you. If you want a reliable spouse, the standard has to be there. If you want to have a close relationship with your children or vice versa, the time must be there. Getting close to God doesn't magically appear, but investing your whole being is required.

We need to fill ourselves with thoughts, people, ideas, and information that will build us up, not pull us down. If you see your progress growing in the right direction, who can not be excited for their future? When you see other people smiling, or hear about their success, you can celebrate them because you know your day is coming as well. When you know what you are carrying—although it may be a baby today, when it is full-grown, wow! What good things will come!

A tree when it is a baby requires a lot and of the chief things, patience. Some trees don't give fruit for 3 years after being planted. Yet, that same tree can live for so many years and give fruit annually with great care. The tree that you started, took care of and gave of your time can feed you, your children, and your grandchildren. We cannot be afraid to make sound decisions that yield great fruit!

We must be a discerner of spirits or people's intentions. We need to be comfortable making sound judgments. Sound decisions lead to what is kept or rejected from your vessel. Being a good judge of character is critical to picking a spouse, friends, and even business relationships. You want to spend your time with people that mutually benefit from the interchange. Be okay with judging situations, circumstances, and yes people. In your judging, however, be fair. To the degree in which we judge, be prepared for the roles to be reversed.

Where we show mercy and grace, we find that we will receive it also. Sometimes we don't get it from those we give it to, but when we need it, it shows up. I have sown seeds in many things and my blessings do not come always from the person I gave them to. I am glad about that because then it would muddy the water if the gift was repayment. I love that you can reap what you sow in all areas of your life.

So, what if your vessel is full or empty what do you do? I love the song title from the music group Xscape, "Who can I run to." I like it because often happy people ask the question who can they run to when they run to when they need love? We are expected to keep the world happy, so who, or what, can keep us happy? Is it possible to fill up when our happiness dwindles to such low depths?

I believe there is a source we can all tap into when we are low. We have someone we can run to when we need to be filled up or our vessel needs emptying. Sometimes we may not know what needs to go because we have grown accustomed to what has been. The who and the what can be summed up like this. The what is your standard of living and how it is defined. We all need a standard that establishes what is good, great, desirable, good, just, etc.

The Bible I believe is the authoritative voice on what is good, being the who. If you look at what is good, you can measure your life, examining yourself to see with God's help what needs to stay or go. This leads me to my next point, the who is the Almighty Yah. Every person on earth is fallible. We are capable of making mistakes. We can change our minds, character, moods, and ideals, and don't always give people notice. People can be flaky and unreliable.

But God! God is our leading Voice and He knows way more than we do. He says that His ways are higher than ours. So why not make Him the Voice of structure and reasoning in our life? Why do we fight coming to God, when we know we run to Him when all our chips are down? The earth turns to God during a crisis, do they not? During 911, for Covid, and other pandemics or catastrophes we find time to seek His face. We make time to plead for His mercy and grace.

We use His likeness to restore HOPE to the world. We use His standards to define LOVE. We are okay with using someone or something, but the struggle comes in when it is time to worship or serve Him. Do we serve Him? Do you serve Him? Will you? Not whenever things go wrong, but when things are going seemingly right?

Being happy is not about being happy only in the moments we enjoy, but about having peace in the moments of trying fire. It is about trusting God's nature, promises, and commitments to help us over our feelings. We must be willing to allow our happiness to be unleashed! We need to use the keys to happiness so that we can obtain and maintain happiness. True happiness is learning to be content in any stage of our promise.

We can only be content with what may seem good or bad if we learn to trust in God. We cannot only trust Him a little or sometimes, but all the time. If your vessel is broken or cracked, He can fill your holes and mend the broken pieces. He has a process that will make you new! If you struggled with eating, your image, issues from your past, thinking you cannot afford to be happy, or living out your fears is more real than your dreams, be encouraged. Help, hope, happiness, and joy have arrived!

You don't have to wait until everything is right in your life to be joyful and happy! You can be happy knowing you are headed now in the right direction. When we are lost, we will never arrive if we travel in the wrong direction. The further we go, the more despair we feel when we are going in the wrong direction. Don't despair! Some of us may have been going in the wrong direction for years now and we are 20, 30, 40, 50, 60, or older. But God is a redeemer of time! God is here to help you get traveling in the right direction. He is more than capable of ordering your steps to get you to your desired and expected end that He planned for you.

Now it is time to implement the keys to happiness. Reflect on the keys from each chapter and allow them to give you a warm hug. When you hear the voice of sound reasoning, which is good judgment, trust the voice and be willing to make the changes to secure your God-centered happiness. When we put first the Kingdom of God and His righteousness, everything else will be added. When we submit our will, to be His will, He will give us the ability to be content in all things. God, Yah, will give you the ability to be and stay happy!

Shalom.

Scriptures to Encourage You

An excerpt to encourage all who have an ear to hear, a heart to feel, a mind to understand, and eyes to perceive, the basis of how being a servant of God is the happiest position—place on earth any man can be. It is the will of Yah (God) for all to come into the wisdom and knowledge of Christ, the Savior of the world, the Lord, teacher, and Master of God's children.

Acts 2:2 - 29
2 I think myself happy, king Agrippa, because I shall answer for myself this day before thee touching all the things whereof I am accused of the Jews: 3 Especially because I know thee to be expert in all customs and questions which are among the Jews: wherefore I beseech thee to hear me patiently. 4 My manner of life from my youth, which was at the first among mine own nation at Jerusalem, know all the Jews; 5 Which knew me from the beginning, if they would testify, that after the most straitest sect of our religion I lived a Pharisee.

6 And now I stand and am judged for the hope of the promise made of God, unto our fathers:7 Unto which promise our twelve tribes, instantly serving God day and night, hope to come. For which hope's sake, king

Agrippa, I am accused of the Jews. 8 Why should it be thought a thing incredible with you, that God should raise the dead? 9 I verily thought with myself, that I ought to do many things contrary to the name of Jesus of Nazareth.10 Which thing I also did in Jerusalem: and many of the saints did I shut up in prison, having received authority from the chief priests; and when they were put to death, I gave my voice against them.

11 And I punished them oft in every synagogue, and compelled them to blaspheme; and being exceedingly mad against them, I persecuted them even unto strange cities. 12 Whereupon as I went to Damascus with authority and commission from the chief priests, 13 At midday, O king, I saw in the way a light from heaven, above the brightness of the sun, shining round about me and them which journeyed with me.14 And when we were all fallen to the earth, I heard a voice speaking unto me, and saying in the Hebrew tongue, Saul, Saul, why persecutest thou me? it is hard for thee to kick against the pricks.

15 And I said, Who art thou, Lord? And he said, I am Jesus whom thou persecutest. 16 But rise, and stand upon thy feet: for I have appeared unto thee for this purpose, to make thee a minister and a witness both of these things which thou hast seen, and of those things in the which I will appear unto thee; 17 Delivering thee from the people, and from the Gentiles, unto whom now I send thee, 18 To open their eyes, and to turn them from darkness to light, and from the power of Satan unto God, that they may receive forgiveness of sins, and inheritance among them which are sanctified by faith that is in me. 19 Whereupon, O king Agrippa, I

was not disobedient unto the heavenly vision:

20 But shewed first unto them of Damascus, and at Jerusalem, and throughout all the coasts of Judaea, and then to the Gentiles, that they should repent and turn to God, and do works meet for repentance. 21 For these causes the Jews caught me in the temple, and went about to kill me. 22 Having therefore obtained help of God, I continue unto this day, witnessing both to small and great, saying none other things than those which the prophets and Moses did say should come: 23 That Christ should suffer, and that he should be the first that should rise from the dead, and should shew light unto the people, and to the Gentiles.24 And as he thus spake for himself, Festus said with a loud voice, Paul, thou art beside thyself; much learning doth make thee mad.

25 But he said, I am not mad, most noble Festus; but speak forth the words of truth and soberness. 26 For the king knoweth of these things, before whom also I speak freely: for I am persuaded that none of these things are hidden from him; for this thing was not done in a corner. 27 King Agrippa, believest thou the prophets? I know that thou believest. 28 Then Agrippa said unto Paul, Almost thou persuadest me to be a Christian. 29 And Paul said, I would to God, that not only thou, but also all that hear me this day, were both almost, and altogether such as I am, except these bonds.

If anyone in the Bible should be entitled to say happiness alluded them it should have been Paul. Paul was a man guilty of many sins, but he was forgiven. In serving God the Father through His Son, our Saviour Yeshua the Christ he suffered many of things. A quick snapshot of his suffering includes:

2 Corinthians 11:24 – 29 Paul talks about his struggles since becoming a bondservant of Christ.

24 Five times I received from the Jews the forty lashes minus one. 25 Three times I was beaten with rods, once I was pelted with stones, three times I was shipwrecked, I spent a night and a day in the open sea, 26 I have been constantly on the move. I have been in danger from rivers, in danger from bandits, in danger from my fellow Jews, in danger from Gentiles; in danger in the city, in danger in the country, in danger at sea; and in danger from false believers.

27 I have labored and toiled and have often gone without sleep; I have known hunger and thirst and have often gone without food; I have been cold and naked. 28 Besides everything else, I face daily the pressure of my concern for all the churches. 29 Who is weak, and I do not feel weak? Who is led into sin, and I do not inwardly burn?
As you can read, life for him was tough! Yet he said this in

Philippians 4:11 - 13:

11 I am not saying this because I am in need, for I have learned to be content whatever the circumstances. 12 I know what it is to be in need, and I know what it is to have plenty. I have learned the secret of being content in any and every situation, whether well fed or hungry, whether living in plenty or in want. 13 I can do all this through him who gives me strength.

The key to our happiness is Christ. He is mighty to save and gives us the power to "think ourselves happy along with the ability to find contentment in all circumstances. May these keys greatly bless your life and you find the happiness you deserve and was created to have since the beginning of time.

Shalom

About The Author

"God blesses those who work for peace, for they will be called the children of God." Matthew 5:9

Krystal Lee is proud to have authored this book and accompanying course to better the lives of readers. She has a heart to help people in their deepest times of need. She writes because she believes there is power in sharing stories and life accounts, that others can benefit and learn from. Sharing is caring, so she shares stories, ideas, and resources to better the lives of her readers.

In addition, Dr. Lee has authored over 20 books across seven or more genres (adult, children, youth fiction, self-help, spiritual growth, novels, and more), in addition to ghostwriting and editing more than 15 published works. She has launched coaching programs, web courses, and helped in the formulation of many startup companies. Her specialty lies in aiding coaches, creatives, and service-based companies in defining their message, brand, unique selling point, client avatar, and generating a sales cycle and structure for her clients.

Empowering individuals is at the core of her

work, and she is driven by her passion to continue writing. In addition to being an author, Krystal Lee is a business owner of multiple companies, a consultant, an ordained chaplain, and a speaker.

For more information about Dr. Krystal Lee or to engage with her further, please scan the provided QR code. To engage with the Coaching series and Monthly Meet up Group for Embrace Your Crown First Sundays at 4pm, please use the QR code or visit KLEembrace.com

FB, TW, IG, TikTok, Youtube:
@AuthorKLee
AuthorKLee.com
DrKrystalLee.com
Me@DrKrystalLee.com
Info@AuthorKLee.com

CONNECT ON SOCIAL MEDIA

Shop Books from AuthorKLee.com

Explore over seven different book genres, and find something suitable for every member of the family.

Scan to Shop All Titles by K. Lee

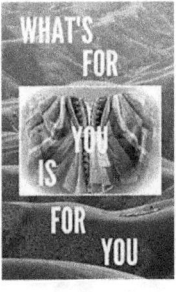

SCAN ME

It's time to start and finish **YOUR Story!**

KLE Publishing specializes in helping people become authors. In as little as 15 to 90 days, we can help you develop your book and publish to 39,000 outlets!

Ghostwrite, Edit, Format, Publish
We can help from
Start to Finish.

KLEPub.com Store

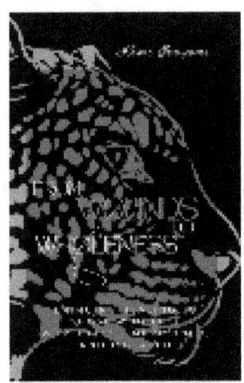

www.ingramcontent.com/pod-product-compliance
Lightning Source LLC
Chambersburg PA
CBHW052109110526
44592CB00013B/1538